Being on the
Oregon Coast

An Essay on Nature, Solitude, the Creation of Value,
and the Art of Human Flourishing

Being on the Oregon Coast

An Essay on Nature, Solitude, the Creation of Value, and the Art of Human Flourishing

SCOTT F. PARKER

THE LITTLE BOUND BOOKS ESSAY SERIES
WWW.LITTLEBOUNDBOOKS.COM

LITTLE BOUND BOOKS
WWW.LITTLEBOUNDBOOKS.COM

Published in 2020 by Homebound Publications
Cover & Interior Designed by Leslie M. Browning
Cover Image: by © Kruse Collins
Interior Illustration by © Chikovnaya

ISBN 978-1-947003-82-8
First Edition Trade Paperback

10 9 8 7 6 5 4 3 2 1

Little Bound Books is committed to ecological stewardship. We greatly value the natural environment and invest in environmental conservation.

For

Parker J. Newton

&

In the spirit of
Parkers Jimmy, Jerry, Johnny

What goes on four feet in the morning,
two feet at noon, and three feet in the evening?

I live my life in widening circles
that reach out across the world.
I may not complete this last one
but I give myself to it.

I circle around God, around the primordial tower.
I've been circling for thousands of years
and I still don't know: am I a falcon,
a storm, or a great song?

    —RILKE

*I give this record of my journey not as
a contribution to human knowledge,
because my knowledge is small and of little account,
but as a contribution to human experience.*

—HENRY MILLER

CONTENTS

About the Author

About the Press

AUTHOR'S NOTE

IN THE LAST DAYS OF SUMMER, I set out for a walk on the Oregon coast. It is not important the route I took, nor the miles I covered. It is not important the number of days I walked, nor the rides I accepted. It is important only that I was on the coast and that I was walking and that I was attempting to carry on a conversation with myself and to inquire of myself what, so far, I had learned.

PREDAWN

YESTERDAY *I LEFT THE CITY* and went into the woods. I strapped my unwieldy pack over my shoulders and took my first tentative steps since the last time. I climbed up through an ancient forest of Sitka spruce and western hemlock—growing since the most recent big earthquake in 1700—on the soft soil of a coastal mountain. Sunbeams from the falling afternoon light pierced the canopy and brought the forest to a mysterious glow. Trees toppled by wind, root systems reaching out like demon tentacles, holes become dens for creatures never seen, moss like heavy drapes between the swaying trees—all the woods rich of nutritious death and decay.

To the west, the great openness of the Pacific that I could just glimpse in the gaps between the trees.

Here it is dark—and just there it is all light.

The late days of summer, the waning hours of the afternoon, low light slanting everything toward sorrow. It is the most bittersweet time, and therefore the most beautiful.

When I reached the first lookout high above the ocean suddenly I could see it all down there, the whole giant thing spread out before me to the end of the world and beyond. Headlands plunging into the water, pocket beaches tucked between them like little art projects. The ocean cyan around the edges, the center of my field of view ablaze with light brighter than color. I looked away and waited for my eyes to adjust.

Somewhere below, a seal barked. I turned back to the darkness and continued on my way.

premise

I am at the coast to do some walking and to answer to myself what I have figured out so far.

It takes time and space to think. And moving through time and space in the outdoors we find these to be expansive. Even if they exist only in the mind, time and space hold us and give our thoughts the opportunity to blossom. We are inside what is inside of us. Metaphysics is full of such paradoxes, but in walking there is only the experience: the slower we move, the longer time extends (if we could be perfectly still we could be immortal); the closer we come to our bodies, the more the world is within our reach.

The momentum of being, just as the momentum of physics, is a scalar quantity. It has speed but knows no particular direction, running along until it collides with another mass and the two are mutually propelled in new directions.

Ever change, ever flux.

The will, a force directing, influencing, propelling, or nudging ever so slightly, but ultimately unable to account for itself. Who—*what*—can?

Solitude too is required for thinking. How else to start listening for one's own thoughts among the cacophony of voices in one's head? An original thought might never appear, but a habitable environment must be offered to the possibility. And when one does appear it appears not as a product from a factory but as a stranger who might become a friend.

Here on the coast, I am alone waiting for surprises. I have left the wasteland of the internet along with my friends and family. Here I will inquire of myself what I know and who I am when the only eyes on me belong not to a lover or a friend, a stranger or an enemy, or even to myself, but to nature—the force that made me, that will destroy me, and that for the time being recognizes me.

4

Of course, I do not travel in complete solitude. I am accompanied by the companions of my thoughts, the relations that occasioned me, and the guides who will help to illuminate my way but who cannot walk it for me. The Oracle of Delphi (know thyself) and the Oracle of Emerson (trust thyself) offer their encouragement, but that is all. The rest is up to me.

Do not mistake the sound of the woods for silence. Listen and the soundscape is full. The wind passing through the trees, the birds rustling in the brush, and the waves crashing in the distance—all of these and more are present underneath the heavy blanket of isolation. The world is a seashell at my ear.

But there is a period of adjustment. The absence of the noises of people at first shouts over the sounds of nature. The ears must adjust, and they will. What's the rush? The relative quiet even of a noisy wood is another burden lifted. The burden of constantly shutting out and ignoring. Of trying not to be distracted by sounds that are intended to distract. Here the sounds are not for me and they are thereby more valuable to me when I am ready to hear them. We are grateful witnesses to a bird's song or the soft rapid patter of squirrel feet across a fallen log.

Far below me last night, as the sun rested on the horizon before sinking once more permanently out of existence, I studied the shapes of a dozen surfers riding the last waves of daylight. Blank figures, anonymous and fully formed, floating, standing, falling, and paddling back out—an ongoing cycle of waves, days, seasons, years, lifetimes. The rhythm of one thing after another playing a part in a larger pattern running from the beginning to the end.

Behind the surfers, the sky swelled golden over the water silhouetting the several rock formations protruding from the sea. From gold to yellow, then red, finally black. The sun, the surfers, the ocean—gone. All that remained were the overflowing moon and the night's first stars.

I pitched my tent in the woods, heeding nothing but those stars.

Those points of light, what are they? And how many over the eons have looked up at them and told stories of everything under them? In our scientific age, the story we tell is of giant balls of burning gas light years removed from the small rock of our planet.

We have unprecedented information about the universe at our demand; nevertheless, when we look up at the stars our information is supplanted by awe. We become reverent like children. Our experience is of wonder, wonder that the universe can be so large, wonder that it should appear so delightful to us, wonder at distance, wonder at light, and finally wonder that any of it should exist at all.

Why is there something rather than nothing?

Who has not asked this question from time to time in moments of idle? And who of our geniuses has yet answered it? The question collapses in our minds under the weight of its own incomprehensibility.

If there were nothing, it would hardly be ours to worry. Conversely, if you can look for existence you are bound to find it. The question is perpetually—inescapably—beyond.

This is the itch I scratch when all else is at peace. Listening to the calling birds and the rolling waves, looking up at the enchanted sky this clear night—how much more likely it seems that nothing would beget nothing and all of this would never be.

Yet as soon as there is something, there has always been something. Any nothing that could produce something was never in a true sense nothing. Perhaps a proto-something, but not a nothing. Nothing is an impossible thought. You can imagine any thing without being: our solar system without Earth, Earth without us, us without any one of us. Things arise and pass away. They come in and out of being, participating in the flux. The flux alone is fundamental.

There is no being without being.

There is no nonexistence, but it does not follow that there could not have been. Things might have been different. They might not have been.

We are monists in this respect: there is being. Need we characterize it beyond recognition?

The universe, by whatever mechanism or method, must be *sui generis*. We think in terms of cause and effect and so want being to be grounded in necessity—but at some point in the infinite regress of existence we come to the limit of our imagination or of our energy and call what remains unexplained the beginning. All the mysteries of science: Why is it this way and not that? What rules account for such effects? How did it come to be so? All of these are subsumed by the questions of why it is at all.

We are finite beings, wisps amidst the infinite. Either we learn how to laugh and go about our affairs, or we somehow learn to think outside the categories of time and space and causality. We are not reduced to wonder, we are elevated to it.

I gazed upward last night until all the divisions evaporated: between today and tomorrow, waking and sleeping, ideas and perceptions. I had solved nothing, but I was at peace with my determination that there was nothing to solve on a peaceful night by the ocean. The mystery of existence, a cause for celebration.

Yesterday I climbed high above the ocean in the thick forest and saw out over the water. Today I will walk on the beach, eye-level with the waves, feet in the sand.

DAWN

WAKE BEFORE SUNRISE, I break camp and begin the day's walk. Around me, trees emerge gradually from the black screen of night. For an instant I catch myself mourning these moments before the physical world presents itself to the senses, when more of it still exists as possibility.

The air is cool and the fog I'm walking in is moderate and will burn off soon. I stop at all the lookouts, recalling my aim not to move fast or cover a lot of ground but to advance with sensitivity. I am walking for a reason: to be where I am instead of rushing forever ahead. I stop at the lookout points and breathe with the waves of the ocean breaking below. It is difficult at first to retrain the skittish mind to stop quantifying experience and wanting to race ahead to the finish.

But a day is a day. In it occurs what occurs. The more I squeeze in the busier and more hurried I become. I want to give my days room to breathe, let them stretch out and become more than a long list of trivial accomplishments. That thing I am all the time rushing toward is all around me and appears as soon as I give up the chase. The things we can think or worry about are inexhaustible and will wear us down to little worry-machines if we let them. Our attention is better spent elsewhere: on the water, for example, the blue expanse—an immensity that restores rather than erodes us.

Even on the trail I'm susceptible to the madness of the race toward death, thinking how many miles can I go before lunch, what if I pick up the pace, what if I eat on the move, what if I forgo breaks, maybe then I can, maybe then I will, and then when I arrive there will be time to spare.

Of course not. The only way to get where you're going is to be where you are. So I stop at the lookout and study the coastline and the way the earth folds on itself and rises up and drops down and then is covered by water farther than my eyes can see. This view never gets old.

So many thoughts fail to cross my mind, including: *This coastline is fine, but why isn't the water a little bluer, why not the rocks a bit more dramatic—then it would be something.*

What a gift we give when we allow ourselves to feel satisfied. What a psychic relief to let go, or just set aside for a little while, the comparisons and feelings of inadequacy we navigate by in our consumer lives. You are in nature when there is nothing for you to buy. I take deeper breaths with this freedom; my footing is sturdier on this ground. A sense of gratitude visits me—for the ocean and the sky, for the land and the trees, and for myself here to participate.

The second miracle is this: that not only is there being, being is aware. It is *like something* to be. Just as something precludes nothing, so consciousness precludes an inanimate universe.

Walking through the woods, I see a cow elk on the path before me. I experience the moment only as I experience it, not as she experiences it.

How could matter give rise to consciousness? And how could consciousness give rise to matter? For two things to interact they must meet somewhere. But for one thing to have two features it need only be looked at in two ways.

I stop to let the elk meander a comfortable distance from the trail before proceeding. I could approach her and wave my walking stick to scare her from my way, but it is her trail as much as it is mine. And I have all the time in the world to wait.

Upslope from the cow is the bull I did not see right away. I am within easy charging distance and he is eyeing me more closely than I would prefer. It is rutting season and I want nothing of an aggressive bull. His eyes are unblinking and unapologetic. He speaks his language, and I speak mine, telling him in a soothing voice to "be cool." He eventually accepts my terms and allows for a peace to develop between us.

When a raccoon emerges from the woods with a sense of purpose and takes the trail, I follow after him, the cow grazing farther and farther down the hill, the bull never moving, never taking his eyes off me.

I have so far been seeing the ocean from above. A great other wrapped around the globe and stretching right up to the shore below me. It takes on metaphysical proportions, this dividing line between land and sea.

On this side, I am free to explore and move about at my leisure. The land presents its hazards to me but is ultimately hospitable. But in the ocean I may never take residence. I may venture in, but if I overstay my welcome I will collide with my limitations. The threat of oblivion lingers out there. This body of water vaster than all the world's land combined.

Naturally, it tempts my approach. Sites of collision are sites of dynamism, occasions for thrill. We are drawn to our limits. We follow the sun and we end up here, on the Pacific coast. The promise that led us here still dangles before us, but from here we can no longer follow. Do we lose faith? Do we continue? Do we turn back?

I get closer. I drop down onto the sand and confront it directly. I remove my shoes and feel the dry sand press up beneath my weight and between my toes. The arches of my feet flex over the wind-driven bumps. The grains of sand are rough and invigorating—they abrade the dead skin and bring me into immediate contact with my environment. The beach grass pricks at my hands and forearms. My steps wisp out loud, spraying sand in the breeze.

Down by the water, my pace quickens on the cold wet sand. Bubbles erupt from the retreating surf. Flocks of seagulls part for my passing. One lone gull turns in from the water and yawns like an animal with nothing to fear. Crab shells are strewn about in staggering quantity. Alongside me the ocean is doing its constant whooshing, the occasional wave breaking and rolling up over my ankles and soaking the hem of my pants. Two gulls pick at a crab that still has meat in its thorax.

Forces colliding give us the world.

It is a thin line between life and death, between consciousness and oblivion. If being were content merely to be it would not be being. An unconscious universe is no universe at all. For whom or for what could it be said to exist? There is no perspective outside perspective, no god outside nature. Undivided reality is no reality at all.

And perspective requires distance. The coast lives where land and water touch. Existence enfolds subject and object alike. The beauty is that these opposites interact, that each makes the other possible. The material and ideal mutually engaged in summoning forth being.

I mean to walk along this boundary line. It is the farthest I can go, so I go right up to the edge. I cross over to test the water, getting in over my head, forcing myself to tread water for a little while. And after I dive in I retreat so that I can recover and prepare myself to dive in again.

My pack is heavy on my shoulders. I have not yet fully adjusted to its weight. And my hip, I can tell, is being rubbed raw where the pack rests against it. That's fine. In time we find freedom underneath our loads. Not everything I carry is strictly necessary, but most of it is reasonable: a tent, a sleeping pad and a sleeping bag, a lamp, a book to read, a notebook to write in, a change of clothes, a rain jacket, a toothbrush, some sunscreen, two water bottles, and a little bit of food. The more we do without the less we find we need.

Yes, we see the world through our own eyes—yet when we see well we see for all. In this way truth is accessible to me now as to all always. There is such a thing. What is my experience then when I look into it? What are its features? What is its essence?

Reality is inside my mind. My body is inside reality. Therefore, my body is inside my mind, which is simultaneously inside my body—both of them spinning. If they cease to spin, I fear, like a top, they will topple.

I cannot rely on the past or on others to be my authority but must be my own. Whatever has been learned I must learn again for myself today. None can walk for me. I take these steps through the woods (following an old Indian path) and now onto the beach (where thousands have gone before me) as if they are original. They are original to me. All experience is unique and the universe sees itself anew through my eyes.

Existence humbles me—the sheer fact of it. I bow before the mystery of being.

What a disappointment if it were to be comprehended.

God's view annihilates. If we somehow knew exactly what literature is and what it is for, it would hardly be worth reading. Just as only an incomprehensible or confounding god is worth worshiping. Let us be grateful for the imperfect, the incomplete, and the limitations that make knowledge and meaning possible—the locality and particularity of consciousness.

Time, space, causality—these are real *to me*. There is no outside space, no before time, no uncaused cause, no view that can see beyond itself.

My world is my imagination, and I make no appeal beyond it.

I follow my thoughts as I follow my legs wherever they lead. The monotonous rhythm of one step after another, the unchanging elements—forest to the east and water to the west, sky above and sand below—I bring myself to leisure. Unhurried, there is time to go anywhere, to veer sideways when I like, to reverse course when I must. The long beach conducive to eternity. It is always here where I am.

MORNING

THE WIND HAS PICKED UP. Wind—the cruelest of the elements.

I wear a target on my chest and the wind is true in its aim. For every resistance it puts against my body it drags double again on my mood. Thankfully, my legs are more persistent than my smile. I will rely on them to maintain my course.

The salt of the ocean adheres to my skin in a sticky film.

The world has turned against me. Perhaps it was never for me.

My footprints are erased in the bluster as quickly as I can leave them. It's as if I am not here, as if I never were.

What can we say? Death is all around and time is running away. The crabs scattered about in pieces. The clamshells, cockle shells, and sand dollars broken apart or sometimes whole, the feathers and every so often the entire gull. The alien globules of expired jellyfish. The snarls of bull kelp and the sand fleas hopping maniacally about them. Just past me now, the stench of a beached seal, body bloated and black with pustules, hard to the poke of my walking stick. Flies in the fur; the birds, who know a thing or two, leaving it to rot in the sun.

I am alone on this walk.

This western edge reminds me that exploration is as much an inner task as an outer one. At any moment the ocean could rise up and swallow me whole. Eventually it will. Meanwhile, I continue.

I did not set out on this journey I am on. Our projects are begun mid-course and defined in hindsight.

We are the children of nature unfolding itself. Our children are the process continued through us.

I have never known where I'm going, have never been the same person at the end of a thought I was at the beginning.

We are the products of decisions made and actions taken by decision-makers and actors who were merely way stations on the regress of being. In living our lives, we conscribe our futures, and in the present moment we discover ourselves conscribed by ghosts from the past.

Power is luck. By chance you have the capacity to create and you create inevitably without knowing how or why or to what end. And by chance one day this power will leave you. We live with the consequences, we live *as* the consequences. I am my own outcome. Ever again this same.

Beings forward and back, we are destinies at some endpoint as we are midpoints of some eventual history.

In a democracy people get the leaders they deserve, and in life people get the character they deserve. I am my father's son; it would be futile to pretend otherwise.

Ahead, my path dead ends. Ocean to the west, cliffs now to the east and running into the water, blocking my route. I will have to backtrack and climb out on the inland side. But tucked in here behind the outcropping of rock I am temporarily shielded from the capricious and tormenting wind.

I sit on a log and enjoy a brief respite before sliding my socks and shoes over my salty, sandy feet and heading back to climb overland.

When did I choose my course? When did I chose my era, my place, my history, and my peers? My self is retrospective. I draw from what needs drawing from so that when I stand here on the beach and say "I" I might mean one thing and not another. That thing may be a necessity, but it is my necessity and I will embrace it and walk the path it set for me in the best cheer accessible to me.

I am a pattern of nature. One way that being has emanated. My backstory only partially knowable, even to myself. Outwardly, I am a being from being. Alive and able. An expression. A creative force.

To create is to take what already exists and alter it. There is no scratch to start from. We are always already begun, forever without originality.

I take my life and I push it in new directions, reach for thoughts that are beyond me, chase the present moment and discover that when I catch it I am perfectly free and that the universe improvises through me. My own creations are not mine—I am an avatar, a medium of their expression. I am freed by this insight. Freed from mistakes, free and spontaneously perfect in life or in death. My song is like a bird's. We are all created, we all emerge from what was before. Apart from the creation, there is no creator. The creator is me, the created. The wave is the ocean, the people the planet, the thought the brain, existence reality.

To be a good guest in this life into which I have been thrown, from which I have emerged one manifestation, to wonder, to follow, to adapt, to make no effort, to not hesitate or interfere—that I call wisdom.

Nature is that which, as the Taoists say, is of itself so. Life indeed comes with a purpose: to go on expressing its nature—to flourish.

Yet very often we quiver before the growth we must allow— it comes at a price—it is a destructive force. But after quivering we commit, and if we're smart we commit just above our capacity. We leap and determine the landing as we fall.

Faith is knowing your entire history has prepared you for this moment, this step on the sand, this wave crashing at your feet, this expression of consciousness, this plumage of being. The path I walk is mine, the walking itself the claim. This shoreline today belongs only to me. Everything I conceive belongs to me, and my imagination is substantial.

But backtracking always portends death, and I am eager still to live. It is a long way back to where a trail can lead me around the outcropping. I climb up an embankment, my pack nearly toppling me back beachward. As the ground flattens I find myself in a stranger's yard. There are no signs of habitants, no dogs, no rifles aimed my way. I look in the window and imagine myself staring back—another me, on a different journey—and am glad to be where I am.

The house is behind me now as I reach the road I will follow south to where I can access the beach again. The detour was slight and the day is still long.

Yes, being is invoked when the thoughts of one particular author have reached their limits. The young man punishes himself for not going farther than he's able. Older, he learns to be content living in the world that is accessible to him (grateful that it is) and trying to do his best with what he has. There is ample room there to move about freely, to wander, to explore, to follow a whim, and to never run out of new territory.

The freedom to invent oneself is always contingent upon the particular sources of our being. And because such sources are unique so too are our flourishings. We must trust our idiosyncrasies because it is only via the same idiosyncrasies that we might doubt them (and thereby reaffirm in practice). Let our theory track our practice when our practice is our given nature.

Walking outdoors our environment can't be abstracted away. The sloppy ground must be traversed. The temperature and likelihood of a storm must be taken into account. The supply of food and water must be carefully budgeted. A protected place to sleep must be scouted. Mind and body find themselves to be allies in the common task of navigating their surroundings.

According to my map, it isn't far to the next town, and I expect to be eating soon. There is no food left in my pack. Carrying only enough for the stretch at hand, I ate my bagel and my apple last night. For now it will be just water until I can find a restaurant for a meal and some coffee. Then I will visit the grocery store and refill my stock with another bagel, another apple, and perhaps—yes, it sounds nice—some nuts.

It is up to us to put down our devices and the shallow connections they entail and wade into the deeper waters of solitude. We are like an amoeba in that we move toward pleasure and away from pain, but pleasure is sometimes a superficial reward, and we differ from amoeba in that conscious self-denial—the highest art—is ever available to us. It is possible for us to reject the easy for the sake of the good that is hard like muscle or wood or poetry. Nature trims us to efficiency. The baggy waste of us excised, the essentials remain: arms and legs, muscles and sinew, clear thoughts and profound trust.

Our honest needs are few: fresh air, clean water, nutritious food, physical movement, intellectual stimulation, and companionship. All flourishing follows from these.

But our attention is no longer our own. We have allowed this invaluable gift to be commodified, and then we have offered it at too cheap a rent. Materially rich and psychically poor, we are an economy of desperate fools. Constant communication has revealed to us nothing so much as how little we have to say.

Our phones fill the gaps in our lives: the time waiting in line at the post office, the moment you look up from your book to let an idea settle, those intervals when you are alone in the world. But we find ourselves in the gaps. Fleeing them, we flee the very spaces in which we might learn to thrive. Technologists promise us that in the future we will be freed up to pursue self-realization, but removed from the external world the self becomes a lonely vessel to navigate a shrinking dominion.

It has not been without anxiety, giving up my iPhone ahead of this walk. But I am so many more gaps now. I am so much space. A great and invisible weight has been lifted.

The short distance to the next town that I read on my map seems now to have been the route by highway. The trail must be closer to six or seven miles, rather than two, all of them climbing or descending. The ground is soggy, this being western Oregon. I have been working my way over this mountain for hours and it will be lunchtime before I eat. My water has run dry now too. But I am not worried. I will make it fine.

I stop at the summit to enjoy the view. When I return to society and revisit the Internet, I will find that I have missed nothing. It will be the same Internet I left behind, with very little to offer me. I will look out a window and see all the passersby, heads bowed to their idiot devices, and I will recall the view from the top of this mountain.

The town is below me now, a long spit of land beyond it running into the bay. It looks like an artist's rendering of a coastal scene under fog. The colors too pure, the lines too straight, the receding land in the distance too proportionally ideal. It is just so. Removing my sweaty shirt and laying it over my pack to dry, I lie against the rocks feeling the sun on my chest. I close my eyes on a windless morning and let the sun light up my closed eyelids. Relaxing after the climb, my mind follows my body to a rare and quiet clarity. I am perfectly still this moment and perfectly capable. My hunger gives me a feeling of vitality. I have seen not one person on this mountain. The cars are far below, and up here is mine alone to enjoy.

I am above the sky. The waves are way down there rising and falling just like a breath, the ocean the lung of the Earth. I breathe it in, too.

We like to compare ourselves to others and induce self-doubt and self-dissatisfaction thereby. We are addicted to this suffering because it is one thing we can rely on to remind us we exist. But the more we are in solitude the more those comparisons drop away. Someone else has received more praise, racked up more quantifiable achievements, gone in whatever way faster or farther than I—well, alone with my own thoughts, walking through a dense forest or along an ancient body of water, self-reproach is hard for me to come by. I might have another's successes if I be another. But for now, the successes available to me are my own. There is no cause for pride or shame. The path I

walk is my own. And at the end of the path, await-
ing my arrival, is the self I have been cultivating
all the while. I meet myself in moments of power,
when I am strong enough to stand where only I
have walked and then to continue walking where
only I can go. Only in being myself may I become
myself.

There are no lies to go on broadcasting, no
fixed identity to go on maintaining. The strictures
of selfhood loosen when the watchman leaves his
post.

The question now is what it is like to be. The phe-
nomenology of *I*—this is the suiology I attempt.
What is a self? And what, specifically, is the one I
have or am?

My consciousness is not the category of consciousness. It is mine, with all its limitations,
and every once in a while without some of them.
I try to grow myself, expand myself, learn more,

know more, be more. If my circle gets big enough its circumference will be beyond my horizon, and still at the center I will find—however it manifests—myself.

Not all nothings are created the same.

So, when I get down to basics, what remains?

I exist only in contrast. Where land and water do not meet there is no shore. I am everything I am not.

The world becomes *for me* the tendencies I have. And my method is to walk myself to exhaustion. Anything I don't carry with me I leave behind. I learn who I am now when I learn what I don't need. We are creatures of necessity and we are capable of significantly more than we realize.

There is strength in self-denial, but strength is a finitude. We reach the edge, as far as the guiding light can lead—and what is left but to trace the limit? And at the limit of self-reinvention, who am

I? At the limit of what any of us can pass, are we all the same? We can go no farther, I can go no farther. We stand mesmerized before the ocean as before the night sky—this species on this planet, trapped or free not according to physics but according to our imagination.

As well as those items in my pack, and even when I put these down, I carry with me my habits, my usual patterns of thought, and the particular ways I have come to understand and engage with the world. In short: not only do I carry my childhood inside me, the man is still the boy. It is by never ceasing to flow that the river of identity exists.

Work, responsibilities, anxiety—they're so far away, so hard to remember. Who am I when these drop away, when I'm alone at the water's edge breathing and walking at an easy pace? Who am I now? It takes an effort to recall that I am anything more than my awareness of the gulls in the sky and the sun on my neck. I am precisely no one as I sit still or walk directionlessly.

We exist in contrast. I create a picture of the light and see myself in the negative. I am no one and nothing unique until I endeavor to interact. Then my *I* comes rushing back with all it entails (my history, my temperament, my mood, my will). Prior to that the subject is passive, receptive, indifferent without being uninterested. I do not move (to get up, to put this pen to this paper, to walk) until I am stimulated to do so, the stimulus being internal far oftener than external.

I stand up to find better shade to sit in only to discover that my legs are hard and stiff from the effort they've given, my calves tight from the mountain. The question of who I am does not arise but in conflict. Who am I? I am of the tired legs. There is no perspective within unity. The subject that abides there may be real, but about it we can say very little. The subject I study is whose company I keep in solitude—the impulses, drives, patterns I have internalized and now orient by. No person is happy who cannot spend days alone in contentment. Wisdom is a rightly measured response. It is an imperviousness to boredom. Those who know it do not create trouble where there is none.

What—or is it who—stays centered when the vicissitudes of life are upon us? If a life is a momentum, self-mastery is the ability to introduce a corrective counter-momentum when necessary—it is also *knowing* what is necessary when. What have I done, but also what have I undone? And what have I withstood?

I am not reducible to any one of my constituent parts. Neither am I their sum. Simultaneously, I am and am not. My boundaries are porous. My identity is fluid. Nature is the way things are, not what I call it.

The self, like everything with a beginning and an end, is amorphous. It is a narrative of various plot points and stylistic touches constantly undergoing its own composition. It is the great unfinished work of each of our lives.

And it evades our scrutiny only in the way the knife cannot cut itself. We do not say of the knife that because it cannot cut itself it therefore does not exist. Nor do we throw our knives in the trash. Rather we use a knife when we would like to cut. Similarly, we needn't be so drastic as to excise the self from our stories because it eludes our attempts to pin it down.

Only dead things hold still.

Variability, slipperiness, and the capacity to frustrate—signs of life.

It seems to me once again that I think best on the move. My legs invigorate my mind, which begins a positive feedback loop of real benefit. When I grow too exhausted to think a new thought

I know it is an honest blankness, hard-earned and deserved.

On my own, my schedule follows the sun's. I lie awake in my tent for no more than an hour after sunset. When I become too tired to read, I flip the switch on my lantern and prepare myself for another morning. I will be up at sunrise, synced up with that ancient and profound cycle.

There are no days of the week here, only sunrises and days, sunsets and nights, ongoing and eternal.

The beginnings and endings of all stories are arbitrary truncations, and the self is no exception.

In the present moment, which is all we have, I am what I value.

The town spread out before me is a welcome sight. My hunger having left my stomach and residing now in my bones, I am ready to take my bounty.

NOON

I NO LONGER DEEM, as I would have at twenty, truth higher than love. It would have been a dishonest report, to be sure, even then; but worse, a foolish objective. Values, first and last.

Walking affords the occasion and the conditions to reflect on our lives: what we care about and how we want to live. What greater challenge is there for us? Walking puts us in the rhythm of the physical body, and compels the mind to follow. We may race ahead of ourselves for a time, but tethered to our feet we are returned to ourselves in due course. Maybe a view or a surprise movement in the trees, perhaps uneven ground or obstacles in our path—our environment insists itself upon us. And free of the Internet, I suddenly have my own thoughts to pursue. The void is easily filled.

We are an adaptable species. The shock of a novel circumstance abates always more rapidly than we anticipate, and we find ourselves going about new business before we are even aware there is business to be done.

And sometimes it is to our benefit to shock ourselves. I replaced my smartphone with a flip phone so that I might keep more regular appointments with myself and cultivate within myself a person content to keep his own company. Anything less than this is to settle for a life that is merely a retreat from death. Even a life that is no life ends in death—only in retreat you ensure your unpreparedness.

The cowardly person hides from death; the reckless person courts it; and the wise person converses with it regularly.

It hasn't taken long for me to lose interest in the news and current events. I can't recall why I spent so much of last week in front of my computer or one thing I looked at there. I recall only the scattered and impatient quality of my attention. I clicked. I felt dissatisfied, so I clicked faster to quell the impatience, but nothing I found to click on was worth my concentration or could counteract the possibility that somewhere out there was what I was really looking for. Days, weeks, lifetimes are lost in this state.

My phone is off. All who can summon me are the ranger across the way if he seeks me and the woodpecker in the tree just to my left, head high, tapping out his curious beat. We live our lives with such access to people and news and culture that the sources are thereby devalued. Sit by the water, walk among the trees—you will miss only the trivia of society and soon will learn you can do without it and indeed are stronger for it. But neglect to sit by water, to walk in woods, to climb on mountains, and you forgo the opportunity to nurture what is best in you.

What news there is, if it means anything, will find me here in the trees, be it yesterday's headline or the heron's squawk.

It is frightening to go inward. Oblivion is there. Death. But as the distractions fade there is nowhere else to go. Nowhere else you'd want to.

Yet even cut off in this way, I am no hermit. Society has been smuggled along with me in the voices in my head.

Madeleines all around me trigger memories that turn into full replays of past relationships. The way the sun shines in September recalls Septembers past, the last days of summer, the longing for it all to be ahead of me yet. I carry all of these memories with me when I walk. Nothing, it seems, turns me toward others like their absence.

I find myself in open conversations with friends, saying things that I have never said out loud and never known I wanted to say. I find myself in arguments about philosophy and politics. I find myself chastising others for not even trying to live up to their own ideals—and hardest always upon myself. I find myself, that is, everywhere but where I am on the beach. It always surprises me how easily I go away again.

But there is more to it. Social creatures, we exist in relation to others. And understanding who we are in our relations brings us closer to ourselves. Alone in the woods, we relate to memories and ideas. Here I am by myself, and yet everyone I care about is with me. Everyone I struggle with is here too, but those I love are better company, and it is to them I reach out. Maybe this is prayer, to feel love in absence. I send such prayers to the sky and am lifted by them.

I am alone and not alone on this walk. Alone, no one else is here. Not alone, without those who are not here now I would not be. I am born of we. The other exists, therefore I am. You bring me into being. You are here with me now.

I drink coffee outside a cafe after lunch and give my legs a little more rest before returning to the beach. The wind has died down and the sky is clear blue. My energy responds to the weather and the food in my belly. I am confident now that I know what I have been pursuing.

We are beings toward meaning. This above all else. Whatever my name, I must answer to myself. To my satisfaction with honest appraisal. We are beings toward meaning where there is none. We are a creative force for meaning. My contingent being is the material of my own perpetual becoming. The reflexive sculptor of self, the values refining themselves.

It is our fate to value. Our highest purpose to value well. The work of a lifetime to know what *well* means.

What is sacred to me? I must answer for myself. It is love and flourishing—these are sacred.

This account I'm keeping of my walk is a testament to experience. It is worth fuel for the fire to me. It is worth one point of contrast to you, one star against which to orient and steer your own ship. The project is the same, but the conditions are ever new.

A report is a reckoning with experience. We must always be prepared to throw ideas and values by the wayside if they inhibit our growth and replace them with new ones. And friends? And friends. To hold on too long is to cling to dead skin. We value growth, but more to the point we grow toward the light of our value. And the dead skin turns to dust.

I read books and am frequently charmed and impressed by them (am a friendly audience)—but how many of them remain in my working consciousness, how many belong to my personal canon? Time strips away all excess. Only those books, those authors—those handfuls of lines!—that resonate with me and with the me I am on the cusp of becoming take a lasting place within. Some of these too will be discarded in turn.

And if I wait long enough perhaps I will even outgrow those I have not yet grown into and eventually be left alone out ahead of my own experience, where it becomes my responsibility to pull myself out of myself—perhaps I am already there. Perhaps we always are.

In the end, is each of us the author of a private canon? Shakespeares for a thousand audiences of one? While we live together, we die alone, and there is only so much we can carry with us to the end. We are beings toward meaning. And what satisfies one will not satisfy another. If everyone's values aligned they wouldn't be values but mere facts. What satisfied me yesterday does not satisfy me today, as today's satisfaction tomorrow will not hold.

What satisfies now? In prolonged solitude we uncover our concerns. I do not miss what I do not need. Walking trims the fat. Along with disposable media output, I am losing my taste for sugar and alcohol already. The elemental me is taking shape. When I cease to struggle with my environment suddenly everything else I need I have or am.

From honest values morality follows—we are creatures toward meaning and some meanings are more valuable than others.

Out here I do not measure the walking days in miles or in dollars. There is no destination but the movement, no measure but the experience.

Either by nature or by (nature in one of its unique forms:) ourselves, we will be wiped from this planet. The most permanent human accomplishments are already being counted down. We live every day unaware of the sand left in the hourglass. Our way of being is impermanent. And it is knowing this intangibility that makes us beings toward meaning. If we knew the time remaining, or if there were no hourglass, there would be no need for value.

But as it is so we walk.

I feel fresh and clear and alive. The salty ocean air has turned to sunlight. How good it feels to be back on the beach and to release my feet from my shoes and let my toes spread and grab at the sand and stretch and flex over the uneven ground. Only a used muscle is a healthy one.

When we plumb the depths of identity our well water is value. We pull the water when we're thirsty but we live above ground.

AFTERNOON

THESE GREAT ROCKS DEPOSITED by the Missoula Flood, these trees all grown since the last big earthquake, the sand made over eons by the ocean, one infinity up against another—the forces here large, and us here trying to be gentle.

I abandon my pack in the woods so I might be light on my feet as I explore this spit of land. These woods are full of deer, and a cougar stalks everywhere I don't look.

On the sand, I walk in bare feet and shorts, carrying only water and my notebook and pen.

Without limits, we are nothing, we do not exist.

Infinite sand, infinite water, singular me.

No man is an island, but we are all standing on the shores of an island at all times. The ocean expresses our common lot in terms prior to language. The perimeter of what is available to us is before our eyes. Standing up, we see even a bit beyond. Yet we will never reach our horizons: they expand with us.

How should I live? *Memento mori*. The rest follows.

This spit is the ideal place to be when a tsunami is not approaching but might. Anywhere else I would preoccupy myself with escape routes. Here a tsunami is just another thing not to worry about. If one comes, all of this land would be submerged and I would be washed away before I could even get halfway back to the base of some high ground to climb.

If I worry helplessly about events beyond my control, the tsunami has already swept me away. I am here on this spit, there is no need to be out at sea. I will drown, but I'm not drowning yet.

If the ocean rises up to take me I will be taken. I will be like the carcass of the gull I just passed.

Tossed about in the surf, washed up and pulled back, inanimate, matter only, subject to the usual forces.

For now I walk ankle deep in the water as long as I can bear it, the cold of the ocean as it comes over my feet shooting pulses up the nerves of my legs. It feels good to step into the relative warmth of the air and the sand. But I go back into the water—the shiver is its own kind of good. The driftwood here is sun-bleached and plentiful. It has floated for years on the open sea and is secured now amidst sea sandwort and orache only for the time being.

Thoughts are like the driftwood, floating on the sea of consciousness and only eventually making land—or not—where they rest exposed to the elements until they are washed away again. They do not know their fate, yet they never fail to follow it.

Only when the storm comes do we discover how secure are our foundations.

I can pass a morning sitting on a log watching the waves and waiting for the sun to break through. This music is conducive to any of my efforts. It plays throughout walking and sitting alike, and it plays for one generation as for the next, it is as close as our kind is likely to come to timelessness on this planet. Eternity is the grains of sand, the series of waves, the horizon, and the sky. It is the miles behind and the miles ahead. It is history and fate. And when I am all thought out I set my stride to the rhythm of the waves and wait to be recharged.

There are two outcomes when you jump out of a plane or into life: either you will die or you will live and then die. I choose the latter.

At the end of the spit are dozens of crab boats. The fishermen pull up their pots and measure their catches, tossing the small ones back for the seagulls, the waves, and their inevitable fragmentation on the sand. Death is constant on the beach. Seeing a lone living crab being harassed by gulls this morning, I scared off the birds and returned it to the ocean—sentimentally, futilely.

On the estuary side are dozens more boats and hundreds more crabs. I follow an inland trail through the woods, but soon it vanishes and I'm left to make my own way through the undergrowth. I duck my head and use my arms to shield my face from branches. My clothes snag on sticks and stickers, a thousand tiny scratches on my arms. I reach an animal trail lined with a variety of scat and innumerable cavities in the thickets for the creatures to hide. It is mid-afternoon, time for rest, yet coyotes howl from not far off as I pass, perhaps as surprised to hear me as I am them. This narrow spit of land is flush with wild. Nature fills all the gaps, and the intricacies of even a small section can engage us as deeply as we are capable of penetrating. The animal trail leads to a side hiking trail and eventually to a main trail. It is there, on the main trail, that I see humans again for the first time on the spit and am reminded how thin is the veil of society.

Wisdom is not knowing much, it is living well. True wisdom is practical. My feet are up, the temperature is just right for the fleece jacket I put on, and the shade is nice—for the moment I have it—we may reject life by distancing ourselves too much from it through analysis and abstraction or we may reduce it to its basest forms through hedonism—or we might really thrive between these in art, in culture, in companionship, and sometimes in solitude.

How should we live? As we would want to have lived. From fifty years off we would be our own judges. When we are compassionate and generous and aimed at virtue, we leave ourselves an inheritance gaining interest. And when we are selfish or cruel we shame the legacies of our estates.

My being is an address to another—and when I'm living well, an address to a friend.

The rules of the game emerge throughout its playing. And to play well is to play gracefully: to do the right thing at the right time in the right way; to be with the world, not against it. Every virtue is only a virtue in relation to its circumstances.

Think of life as a project of meaning and there is always a way to participate, always something to contribute: a deed to be done, a feeling to be shared, kindness to be extended, forgiveness to be granted. But think of life as a property and you will spend your life vainly patching holes in fences. If life understands itself in opposition to death, death—because it will win—has already won.

Let us care for sources as well and as much as for products. The philosopher who would be a happy brain in a vat should be reminded that the vat rests on the same ground his body might have moved over, had he feet to stand on. Greatness is a pyramid whose foundation is nature and whose apex is nature too.

Therefore, the consumer is the lowest form of human. It is a being so starved of meaning and so devoid of imagination that it flees from death through acquisition, as if opposing oneself to one's environment didn't cripple both.

I hear an echo from the woods as I sit facing the sea. If it is worth watching for whales when they are passing by, surely it's worth watching when they aren't.

There is no difference now between gray and blue—even the rocks in the ocean are shades of these. It is so very quiet an animal rustles some leaves and the whole forest leans in to attention. There are so many things in the world about which I am not thinking as I sit here. Where nothing is in conflict, nothing is brought forth. I am looking out over a great sleeping world, content, unmoved, patient.

But even now in the calm, I know a storm is brewing somewhere in Alaska and sooner than that someone will stumble upon my idyll. And I will be jarred into action—the hike back through muddy woods to camp. Are the clouds breaking up? No. Are they? Perhaps, yes. A little.

It is not that language is inadequate for expression. Language is the way things are said. It is that language is antithetical to silence. And silence is the way things are unsaid.

When the rains come, I venture out into them. I zip up my jacket and go on. The mountains and the sea, if they are still there, are occluded by the clouds. The air is saturated with wetness all pervasive. The ocean becomes a three-dimensional fact. I am the ocean gray, the gray that lingers.

But soaked through pants and socks, I am strong. Indomitable. Traveling by foot provides the body an animal confidence—I am that confidence embodied. Balance and strength and energy are mine alone. I have access to stores of power that rain cannot dampen. I jump a puddle. It might have been a pond. I greet the rain. It might have been a friend.

TWILIGHT

I T'S NOT DARK YET. From the lookout, I can see all the way I've come so far: the beaches, the rocks, the capes, the constant presence of the ocean.

I pause a moment to consider my journey and discover fond feelings for the person who began it. The ground between has been the site of struggle and triumph, and I am fond of who walked there as well. Tracing the way to where I now stand, I meet a happy soul wearing my shoes.

And yet in having been brought to hindsight I have simultaneously been brought to foresight as well. The end is fast approaching.

I raise my pack from the ground and swing it over my shoulder. Comically, the momentum ejects the water bottle from the outside netting of the pack. It clangs against the rocks. I stand helplessly as the bottle rolls in slow motion toward the ledge and over. A tree root delays but cannot halt the fall, and the water bottle disappears into the wall of the cape below.

In retrospect we see easily our past mistakes, yet we cannot imagine except in the abstract that we mistake now. If we could in any specific case, we promptly would cease to. My politics were misguided but now they are correct in every detail. If my faith is mislain I shall never hear of it—only in some future shall I hear with amusement of the lesser views of this lesser creature.

But we believe too easily in progress. If time and space are the bounds of thought, and causality the rule of the game, progress is the faith that the game is rigged to always produce a winner. But I've seen too many players holding too many losing hands and very few who have learned to celebrate the game itself above its outcomes.

The highest truth for an individual, a species, a planet, a history is contingency. Nothing is promised, everything is sacred, the game doesn't end even when all the players stop playing—these become merely the game's latest conditions. The universe is as big and as interesting as my cultivation. It will grow as long as I will. And it will shrink as I let myself shrink. It takes energy to grow and as like attracts like the energy repays in kind. The rewards of life are inherent and self-reinforcing.

We hear of the man who drops dead the day after his retirement, having found himself suddenly for the first time with nothing to do. With more sympathy, we hear of the man who drops dead of a broken heart soon after his partner in life has passed. Don't we also sometimes hear of a man who on his last day has more purpose than on any day prior. When he drops dead it is in the middle of some noble pursuit. His friends and family are shocked, but upon brief reflection discover themselves incapable of regret. This man did not resist death or fear it—but in a way he was acquainted with it. Death is inevitable, his actions announce to us, and the only waste of life is to pretend otherwise.

One must be engaged with the world in order to retreat from it for reflection. Without engagement, no world. There is no reflection as such, no ghost in the machine, no Descartes in the chamber.

I have seen something here on the coast. It is clear to me when I wade out into the ocean, when I float past the break, when I ride the waves back in, when I walk on the sand with the sun on my back, it is clear in my body, in my actions, in the thoughts I have when I'm moving. Walking through the woods or running through the beach grass, there is nothing that needs justifying. Yet always there remains a witness to my events. Every moment of being is an account to myself.

We live all the time bounded by the limits of our thoughts—except when on occasion we escape them and are made dizzy again with possibility and infinite energy.

We acquire truth through experience. Education is exposure. Books are for inspiration, to point the way back to experience. They are true insofar as they lead the way, false insofar as they merely appease taste. It is more important that an idea bring good effects than that it achieve consensus. Every idiot speaks the truth now and again. The teacher brings about greater confidence in his skeptical audience, among whom he is fortunate on occasion to count himself. And he brings these about through dynamism of spirit, which he feeds the fuels of good food, vigorous activity, intellectual engagement, honest fellow-feeling, and above all love for the world.

If the universe is a balloon, I inflate it with my optimism. One day it will be nothing. But there will be other optimisms and other universes. For the time being what I have are experiences—experiences of the world, of consciousness, of myself, of loved ones, and of loved places—and the experience of gratitude for the facts of these things when I cannot penetrate their causes. I am grateful for this life. And I testify to experience because experience is what I have to share.

Though my footprints are blown away in the wind, something of me leaves a trace.

But when I cease to break trail I begin to decay. If I stop for an afternoon instead of an hour my mood ebbs, as do my thoughts. The two are the same and grow stale and slack in sloth. I call virtue a reluctance toward slackness. True leisure is active. There, better thoughts and better moods enter me. The energy of the legs is contagious to the soul. It is wise to rest when rest is needed. It evinces a lack of self-respect to rest when rest is unneeded. My statue of a thinker is a human being mid-stride.

The blue ocean of the summer afternoon is the same gray water of winter storms. I am like the ocean—now exuberant, now melancholy, ever myself.

Were it all payoff, experience wouldn't be worthy of truth. You register for the struggle. You volunteer for some suffering ahead of time such that when it arrives you must simply bear it out. If some strength of character comes to me it will come from the self-denial I have imposed upon myself.

Yet I am tired. And tired, I become a stranger to myself. A loneliness comes over me. It is a spiritual fatigue not a physical one. The body is tireless, but the soul requires injections of life.

I can't remember why I am here or what I had hoped to accomplish. I need something—some-one—to unburden me from myself. The hardship of solitude is that positive emotions are magnified in intimate company and negative emotions lessened. Nothing is as beautiful as when it's shared. And nothing more painful than when kept private.

From the beach, the sun low on the horizon, I take out my phone and finally call Sandy.

I tell her that I'm by the water and that the sun is setting. I tell her the inland sky is indigo over the dunes, and I wish she could see it.

I tell her that I almost didn't call but that I'm glad I did because it's nice to hear her voice. I tell her it's late in the day, late in my walk, and that I'm feeling lonely

I tell her the hills here have all been denuded.

I tell her I like to imagine watching this beach in time-lapse: there's a forest, the humans cut it down, then it grows back. The clear cuts are just blips on the screen as the coastline changes. I can find solace in that.

She asks if it is still light out.

I tell her barely. The sun is half under. There's no way I'll make camp before dark. But I don't mind. The day is wondrous.

We say goodbye and I watch the sun go down.

I must follow my impulses and have faith that my impulses will prove discerning. I followed the impulse to visit the coast, the impulse to be alone, and now the impulse to call Sandy. If I would rely on myself, I would rely, then, on the self that sometimes relies on others. If my nature is wise, it is as wise in its communion as in its autonomy.

It is the same with discourse as it is with walking: follow the path that looks most promising, abandon those not bearing fruit and linger on those that are. There is no hurry.

In the woods, I see history: a cedar and a spruce that once grew together. As the faster-growing spruce outcompeted the cedar for resources the cedar died. It clings now to the side of the spruce. I have my own skin to shed. I have my own scars.

Everything I think and know, I think and know in this body with this history moving through this geography.

We are animals first. Thoughts and language are luxuries quickly expunged. So when they are available to us, we do well to seize and create from them. We must earn our selves as well as our projects. There are no easy assurances. In all our pursuits death stalks.

I walk alongside the foreign body of water. At a moment it could sweep me from existence or I could enter into it and disappear myself. Death tempts as well as stalks.

Nature in its scale reminds us that we will all be returned to the source. We are decentered. Not everything is by us or for us.

There are no solipsists along the ocean.

NIGHT

AFTER SUNSET BUT BEFORE THE DARKNESS of night, it's beach and sky as far ahead as I can see, a white wall of fog between them. I run and run and nothing changes. I look behind me and it is the same. I am in the middle; the beginning, as well as the end, lost to me. No reference to how far I've come or how far I have yet to go. The residual light is fading and I fear that I will become lost in the night. I am way out on the beach from camp and I don't know how far there is still to go.

I clutch my flip-flops in one hand and my notebook in the other and run for mile after repeating mile. The point I walked to was twice as far as the woman on the beach told me and now I'm out of light. Isn't this the way. But as long as I keep the ocean on my right and don't go too far I have only to be patient.

Axiology. Philosophy is about the highest things and the highest things are values. What we value: how we live.

Whoso would be my philosopher must be my friend—one who offers not prescriptions but fellowship. She is at my side (and maybe just a bit ahead) fighting the fight for meaning, sharing my concerns and interests and leading me beyond them. Someone who by pursuing her own inquiries helps me to pursue mine. I call out blindly in the dark. If there is a companion out there for the journey the companion will answer.

Emerson and Nietzsche and Chuang Tzu and Lucretius—these are my tribe. My voice is the way their voices mix inside the facts of me. My thoughts, my concerns, my commitments do not belong to me. I am but the iceberg above water; they are the iceberg below. I am but the wave rising up now; they are the whole ocean from which I rise.

First there is the world. Then there is perception of the world. You must ask yourself who you are. You are your values. Your values determine how you live. And you live with others. In a world of Culture. And Nature.

That is: your awareness starts out of the world and gradually moves inward until it sees its reflection in the mirror of self and gradually returns to the world *altered*.

What is different? You are always already yourself. What you may gain is your acquaintance. Nature and Culture remain as they were, nature and culture, but now they are the wellsprings of meaning. You look at the stars in wonder still, but these same stars now, too, are alive. Two birds fly so low to the water their wings might touch the surface. Life is animated with meaning.

In metaphysics, momentum; in epistemology, humility; in selfhood, cultivation; in ethics, virtue; and in aesthetics, meaning.

The quiet before dusk this afternoon was rare and precious. The ocean's muffled roar floated in through the far-off mouth of the estuary. The end of summer was all around—the end of summer always my favorite sadness.

Our thoughts are turned backward as we prepare for the gradual settling in of fall and winter. It is a good time for adventures to end and for adventurers to return home to loved ones and commitments and the ties that bind us to people and place. It was so still, so calm. I sat cross-legged a few feet from the water's edge. I looked out to the ocean I've looked out to so many hundreds of times before. The past was so close, as if it were still going underneath the present.

It is natural to look back from the end just as it is natural to look forward from the beginning. In our own lives we are always simultaneously at the end and the beginning. We can look forward and back as well as all around and it is important to look everywhere we can see—we know not where the truth resides at any time.

There were no clouds over the ocean. I knew it wouldn't last. But I knew, too, that it would come again.

The earth will be okay whether it be home to us or not. People, like populations, are held in check by limits they cannot see until they trespass them. We can breach these limits for the short run, but in the long run there is a corrective force that restores a tenuous balance.

What are we aimed at and how do we achieve our aims? To what do we give our time, our energies, our thoughts, our creativity, our passion? Nature is history and destiny. We live well when we accord ourselves with it, when we express our nature through acts and deeds. We resist our own suffering. Nature rewards the actor who plays his role and doesn't steal lines. Doing the right thing in the right way at the right moment—that is grace, that is embodied wisdom. Just as the wave never breaks on the wrong shore and the bird never sings the wrong note, we do no wrong when we follow nature.

I gave a good scare to a small group of people on the beach building a bonfire. The silhouette of me running out of the darkness and back into it. They never saw me coming, they never saw me go.

Now I turn up from the beach in what I hope is the right spot. By the moonlight I make my way from one tree to the next until I chance upon my tent.

I have no more food. I have no fire. I am cold. My back is sore from carrying my pack. I drink the last of my water.

Inside the tent, I lie down. I am enveloped by blackness, but I think of the ocean and the soft sky, the lavender-touched clouds at sunset and

the trees swaying in the breeze. It is my preroga-
tive to see beauty all around me.

I don't want to get to the bottom of anything—
the bottom, as well as the top, are for the young. I
want to be in all things on the human scale, I want
to think and do human things. The only questions
that mean anything to me are what to value and
how. The rest is commentary.

TOMORROW

THE WORLD IS SO QUIET SOMETIMES I wonder if it exists.

The air is cold. Fall is abruptly upon me. I put on my gloves and my jacket and nestle into my sleeping bag.

I won't sleep well, but no matter. As I am tossed between dreaming and waking, the ocean will be with me in consciousness. I can hear it in the sound of my own mind humming: its constancy, its assurance, its threat, its sacredness. The water is inside me.

Cold, not tired, I will rise early, layer my clothes, and walk myself warm. My fingers won't work right but they'll work well enough and they will come to life as the day goes on. There will be half a white moon in a brittle blue sky. Fog will be sitting densely over the bay as I pass, placid green hills behind.

Tomorrow on the beach at sunrise I will meet a man, a devout man with a deep satisfaction about him. We will talk and he will say he has come down to the sand to pray and I will understand, and he will point to the sea and I will look where he looks, and he will invite me to see as he sees and part of me will be drawn along with him. Do I know God loves me? In some sense, I do. And I know that attending to God's love can engender humility and compassion and gratitude. When I look for good I find it.

Together we will admire the ocean and let the sublime wash over us. Then the man will produce a stack of cards and tell me that not only does God love me but the Word of God is the answer to all of my questions.

I will accept the cards as a gift and promise to read them. Later, when I do, I will encounter small ideas on small pieces of paper—a most plainly man-made and self-indulgent story told: the faithful and the unfaithful, the saved and the damned, God a vain and foolish fantasy; they will have nothing on the analogy of the man on the beach when he points out to the ocean and says God is vast and incomprehensible.

A mile or two after parting with the religious man, I will come to a steep dune I must climb to get over an outcropping and continue my journey. I will make tracks up its face one trifling step at a time, my feet under my pack sliding back as the sand gives way beneath me. I will advance incrementally and happily. I will face the sun as I approach the summit, my walking stick supporting me. When I reach the top of the dune and pause to wipe the sweat from my brow I will look down from my height and see again on the far side of the outcropping the surfers out there in the water, bobbing half-submerged, content in their wait.

When the right wave comes each in turn will rise up from the water and ride the swell balanced on the precipice of the break. When they wobble from the course the fall is sudden, but when they ride on the fine line between the not-yet ahead and the destruction at their heels, their tribe worships being without analysis. They embody what the poet expresses, their activity direct, their creativity honest, their celebration sincere.

There is nothing a surfer riding a wave needs explained. They know what it means to be a human being with nothing promised to no one, no saving or not saving, no time but now, this rock we cling to and when we're feeling bold let go of, this rock mostly covered by water, this rock our home, in these conditions our limits, our life, our chance for something original this wave or the next, tomorrow or another day.

I will watch these surfers from above and when I have stood long enough I will run down the far side of the dune and if I do not stumble I will make it once more to where the water meets the land.

Being is mattering.

We are beings toward meaning. Our duty is to make meaning, to go on expressing nature through culture. And as experience makes expression possible, so too does expression expand experience. We know *that* we are making but not always what—we follow impulses, we trust they will lead us to where we don't yet know we are meant to be. The process, the journey, leads us to new, unimagined possibilities, to new meanings. We always are moving toward some provisional end of which we can never conceive, leaving behind some future past.

Two billion years ago, my ancestors emerged from this water so that today I might walk on this beach.

When I stand here and stare into the ocean, does the ocean stare back?

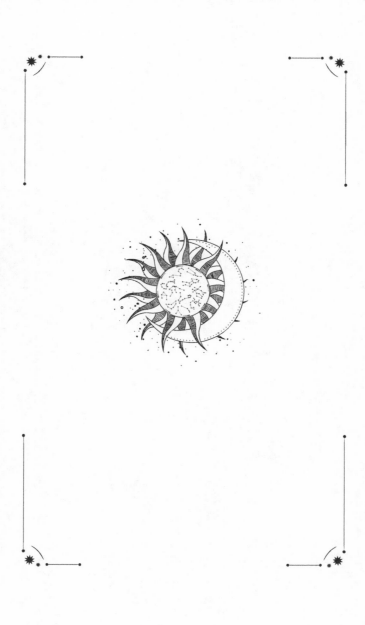

A BOUT THE AUTHOR

Scott F. Parker is the author of *A Way Home: Oregon Essays* and *Running after Prefontaine: A Memoir* as well as the editor of *Conversations with Joan Didion*, *Conversations with Ken Kesey*, and *Coffee— Philosophy for Everyone: Grounds for Debate* (with Mike W. Austin). His essays and reviews have appeared in *Tin House, Philosophy Now, Sport Literate*, and *Rain Taxi*, among other publications. Parker lives in Bozeman, Montana, with his wife and son. He teaches writing at Montana State University.

LITTLE
BOUND BOOKS